To:

From:

WISDOM FROM

RANDOM ACTS OF KINDNESS

By the Editors of Conari Press

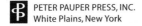

PETER PAUPER PRESS, INC.
White Plains, New York

For Anne Herbert,
the woman who started the movement

The text in this book is excerpted from
Random Acts of Kindness
The Editors of Conari Press
Originally published by Conari Press
Copyright © 2002, 1993 by Conari Press

Published in 2012
by arrangement with Conari Press.

Designed by David Cole Wheeler

Peter Pauper Press, Inc.
202 Mamaroneck Avenue
White Plains, NY 10601
ISBN 978-1-4413-0734-7
Printed in China
7 6 5 4 3 2 1

Visit us at www.peterpauper.com

WISDOM FROM

RANDOM ACTS OF KINDNESS

LIVING FROM THE HEART

When I was small my grandmother told me, "When you give from here [she pointed to her solar plexus], it's like keeping a ledger book. That's not giving, that's trading. I give you three so you give me three. You give your soul away when you give like that. Giving is supposed to be from here," she said, pointing to her chest. "When you give from your heart, it's not so you get anything back. You give because you want to. When you give like this, it fills you up. Your heart can never run out. There are no strangers. And remember to notice when other people give to you like this. Be sure to thank them."

Decades later, struggling with a life-threatening disease, I traveled to a conference in search of answers. Poet Maya Angelou, one of the speakers, told of surviving a childhood of terror and violence. Her handholds through the darkness were gifts of beauty from favorite authors and artists. "Their work inspired me, shaped my thinking, exposed me to what could be possible," she recalled. "And I have never forgotten to say thank you for those random acts of kindness." Maya Angelou's words left fingerprints on my heart as if it were warm wax.

Once you begin to perform and acknowledge random acts of kindness, you no longer believe what you do does not matter. It is as if you're dancing along a beach, making footprints where the shoreline meets the sea. You know the tide will come and wash away the marks your dance has left. Still, it lives on in your heart, as does the delight of being alive. You know you make a difference.

Warning: Acknowledging random acts of kindness in your life, be they in nature, works of art, moments of truth, rescue, or redemption, will bind you to them. The tough shell around your heart will crack ever so slightly. The circumference of who you are will swell full and ripe. It is our hope you will be inspired by what we have breathed into these pages, and you will practice random acts of kindness, so that which came to you as seed will pass on to the next as blossom, and that which came to you as blossom will go on as fruit.

Dawna Markova, Ph.D.

SPARE CHANGE

Every day I walk down the mall to get a cup of cappuccino, and every day I get hit up for spare change. Every day. The panhandlers all have these wonderful stories but you never know what to believe. After a while it gets to be an irritation, and then I find myself getting upset that I'm so irritated over what is really just spare change. One day this person came up to me and said, "I just ran out of gas. My car is about six blocks away from here. I have two kids in the car and I'm just trying to get back home."

I said to myself, "Here we go again," but for some reason I gave him $10. Then I went on and got my cappuccino. As I was walking back to my office, I again saw the man standing by his car, which had run out of gas right in front of my office. Seeing me, he came over and said, "Thank you, but I don't need the full ten," and handed me $2.

Now I find that being asked for money no longer bothers me and I give whatever I can every time I get the chance.

THE MAGIC DRAGON

Several years ago, when I was living in Chicago, I read in the newspaper about a little boy who had leukemia. Every time he was feeling discouraged or particularly sick, a package would arrive for him containing some little toy or book to cheer him up with a note saying the present was from the Magic Dragon. No one knew who it was. Eventually the boy died and his parents thought the Magic Dragon finally would come forth and reveal him or herself. But that never happened. After hearing the story, I resolved to become a Magic Dragon whenever I could and have had many occasions.

If there is any kindness I can show, or any good thing I can do to any fellow being, let me do it now, and not deter or neglect it, as I shall not pass this way again.

—WILLIAM PENN

PRACTICE RANDOM ACTS OF KINDNESS!

• Spend half an hour in a hospital emergency room and do one random act of kindness that presents itself.

• Offer to help people who could use the assistance to cross streets—seniors the blind, small children. . . .

• The next time someone speaks to you, listen deeply without expecting anything.

• Plant a tree in your neighborhood.

❀ – ⭐ – ❀ – ⭐ – ❀ – ⭐ – ❀

• Find someone you've been close to and sit back to back with her. For a few minutes disclose the random acts of kindness she has done for you while she just listens. Then switch and listen to the wonderful things you have done.

• Yes, it's a drag, but why not put your shopping cart back in its appointed place in the parking lot?

• Write a note to the boss of someone who has helped you, thanking him or her for having such a great employee.

THE FORGIVEN DEBT

I had a client who owed me a good deal of money. Eventually she stopped seeing me, but each month I would send her a bill and receive no response. Finally I wrote to her and said, "I don't know what difficulty has befallen you that you are unable to pay me, but whatever it is, I'm writing to tell you your debt is forgiven in full. My only request is that at some point in your life, when your circumstances have changed, you will pass this favor on to someone else."

I am of the opinion that my life belongs to the community, and as long as I live, it is my privilege to do for it whatever I can. I want to be thoroughly used up when I die, for the harder I work, the more I live. Life is no "brief candle" to me. It is a sort of splendid torch which I have got hold of for a moment, and I want to make it burn as brightly as possible before handing it on to future generations.

—GEORGE BERNARD SHAW

A Bouquet of Flowers

When I graduated from college I took a job at an insurance company in this huge downtown office building. On my first day, I was escorted to this tiny cubicle surrounded by what seemed like thousands of other tiny cubicles, and put to work doing some meaningless thing. It was so terribly depressing I almost broke down crying. At lunch—after literally punching out on a time clock—all I could think about was how much I wanted to quit, but I couldn't because I desperately needed the money.

When I got back to my cubicle after lunch there was a beautiful bouquet of flowers sitting on my desk. For the whole first month I worked there flowers just kept arriving on my desk. I found out later that it had been a kind of spontaneous office project. A woman in the cubicle next to me brought in the first flowers to try to cheer me up, and then other people just began replenishing my vase. I ended up working there for two years, and many of my best, longest-lasting friendships grew out of that experience.

❀ – ★ – ❀ – ★ – ❀ – ★ – ❀

A GIFT OF FEAR

Two days before my fiftieth birthday I had a heart attack. It was a most surprising random act of kindness. I had lived the previous thirty years of my life as a powerful, successful, and amazingly productive man.

I had also lived so cut off from my emotions that I couldn't even fathom what the whole fuss about feelings was all about. I had worn out the efforts of three good women, took pride in my unfeeling logic, denied that there was anything wrong or missing in my life, and was prepared to march stubbornly forward.

Until I was felled and terrified by my own heart. That experience unlocked a lifetime of buried emotions. So, without knowing it, when the doctors revived me, they delivered me to a life fuller and more beautiful than I had ever imagined.

If you bring forth what is inside of you, what you bring forth will save you. If you don't bring forth what is inside of you, what you don't bring forth will destroy you.

—JESUS

THE OLD DOG

I used to jog through the park every morning, and I always went by an old woman who sat on a bench with a small, very old, mangy dog. One day I noticed her dog wasn't with her. For some reason I stopped and asked her where he was. Suddenly, tears started running down the lines in her face and she told me he had died the night before. I sat and talked with her for over an hour. Every day after that we would greet each other as I came by; sometimes I would stop and talk with her for a while. She was very lonely but also very strong, and to this day I

think of her when I'm sad, and it
makes me smile.

We cannot live only for ourselves.
A thousand fibers connect us with our
fellow men; and among those fibers,
as sympathetic threads, our
actions run as causes, and they
come back to us as effects.

—Herman Melville

PRACTICE RANDOM ACTS OF KINDNESS!

• Make a list of things to do to bring more kindness into the world and have a friend make a list. Exchange lists and do one item per day for a month.

• Spend a week just being aware of things in nature that befriend you.

• Hold a random acts of kindness party where everyone tells the stories of kindnesses in their life.

• Bring a little beauty into sterile places—drop off a geranium plant at a police station or a cutting from a houseplant to your local fire station.

❀ – ⭐ – ❀ – ⭐ – ❀ – ⭐ – ❀

• When someone is trying to merge into your lane in traffic, let him in— and why not smile and wave while doing it!

• All of you reading these words have loved someone, have done someone a kindness, have healed a wound, have taken on a challenge, have created something beautiful, and have enjoyed breathing the air of existence. Never doubt how precious, how vitally important you are. Every moment you make a difference. So, today, appreciate yourself as a random act of kindness.

An Unexpected Apology

I was driving home from work one day and the traffic was terrible. We were crawling along and out of nowhere this guy just pulls out onto the shoulder, passes a whole line of cars, and cuts me off so quickly I have to slam on the brakes to keep from crashing into him. I was really rattled. About fifteen minutes later, I'm stopped at a light and I look over and there is the same guy next to me, waving for me to roll down my window. I could feel my adrenaline starting to flow and all my defenses coming up, but for some reason I roll down the window, and he says, "I am terribly sorry. Sometimes when I get into my car I become such a jerk. I know this must seem stupid, but I am glad I could find you to apologize." Suddenly my whole body just relaxed and all the tension and frustration of the day, the traffic, life just dissipated in this wonderfully warm, unexpected embrace.

Compassion is an alternate perception.

—M. C. RICHARDS

Amazing Grace

We had just searched a small village that had been suspected of harboring Viet Cong. We really tore the place up—it wasn't hard to do—but had found nothing. Just up the trail from the village we were ambushed. I got hit and don't remember anything more until I woke up with a very old Vietnamese woman leaning over me. Before I passed out again I remembered seeing her in the village we had just destroyed and I knew I was going to die. When I woke again, the hole in my left side had been cleaned and bandaged, and the woman was leaning over me again offering me a cup of warm tea. As I was drinking the tea and wondering why I was still alive, a helicopter landed nearby to take me back. The woman quietly got up and disappeared down the trail.

What good will it do you to think, "Oh, I have done evil, I have made many mistakes"? It requires no ghost to tell us that. Bring in the light, and the evil goes out in a moment.

—VIVEKANANDA

Pass It On

During the Depression my grandmother was a society matron in Cleveland and, as she put it, "quite taken with myself." One morning she found a basket of food on her doorstep. It made her furious—how could anyone think that she was some poor needy person? Not knowing what to do, she put the basket in the kitchen without even bothering to unpack it. The next morning another basket of food was on her front step. By the end of the week she had five food baskets beginning to clutter up her immaculate kitchen, and she decided that the

※ – ⭐ – ※ – ⭐ – ※ – ⭐ – ※

east she could do was to pass the food
along to those who were really needy.
The baskets continued to arrive for a
couple more weeks, and my grandmother realized that she had begun to
look forward to her part in helping
find someone who needed them.
When the morning deliveries finally
stopped, she starting making her own
food baskets to give away.

The moral of the story? Said my
grandmother, "Someone knew I really
was a poor needy person and found
the best way possible to help me."

SEEING THE SKY

I live high in the hills and my body is getting old. One day I was out in my garden fussing with weeds and grew tired. I decided to lie back on the grass and rest like I used to when I was a small boy. I woke up some minutes later with a neighbor whom I had never met leaning over me, all out of breath, asking me if I were OK. He had looked out his window two blocks up the hill and saw me lying on my back on the grass, looking, I am sure, like the victim of a stroke or heart attack, and had run all the way down the hill to check on me. It was embarrassing but it was also so wonderfully touching. After we had it all sorted out, he let out a deep breath and lay down on the grass beside me. We both stayed there very quietly for a while and then he said, "Thank you for deciding to take your nap out on the lawn where I could see you. The sky is such a beautiful thing and I cannot remember the last time I really looked at it."

Practice Random Acts of Kindness!

• Write a letter of appreciation to that which in nature has been a safe place for you.

• As you go about your day, why not pick up the trash you find on the sidewalk?

• Give another driver your parking spot.

• If you are in any of the helping professions, ask your clients to tell you their stories of random acts of kindness

A traveling salesman we know always carries cracked corn in his car and scatters it for birds during the snowy winter months.

On Thanksgiving, call up everyone you know and ask them what they are thankful for so they can feel their own gratitude.

Talk to people at work about one of your random acts of kindness and ask about theirs. Disclosure stimulates us to do more by emphasizing the pleasure of giving with no strings attached.

THE SKIING ACCIDENT

When I was about 19 or 20, I was skiing down a mountain when I saw a woman who had fallen. She was clearly hurt and crying and trying to get up, but she couldn't. So I flagged down somebody to get the ski patrol and stayed with her, talking to her, holding her hand, touching her shoulder. It was the last run of the day; it was getting really cold and snowing hard. About a half hour later, the ski patrol showed up and took her down the mountain. I stayed with her because she was so scared. She kept saying, "I think there might be somethin wrong." I said, "Well there might be. I'll make sure you get the care you need." Finally the ambulance came and took her to the hospital. I guess her leg was broken in about four places. I never saw her again, but it was clear my presence was important to her. I know that's true.

To receive everything, one must open one's hands and give.

—TAISEN DESHIMARU

Two Flat Tires

I used to make an eighty-mile drive to visit my parents. One forty-mile stretch of the road is in the middle of nowhere. One day as I was driving alone along this barren patch, I saw a family on the side of the road with a flat tire. Normally I do not stop in such situations, but for some reason I felt the need to do so that day. The family was very relieved when I volunteered to drive them to a gas station about ten miles down the road to get help. I left them at the station because the attendant said he would take them back to their car and drove on my way

About twelve miles later I had a blowout. Since I couldn't change the tire myself, I was stranded and not sure what to do. But in only about ten minutes along came a car and it pulled over to offer help. It was the same family I had stopped for earlier that day!

This only is charity, to do all, all that we can.

—JOHN DONNE

WORDS OF COMFORT

I was walking up Amsterdam Avenue in New York during a particularly dark time of my life. I had recently lost a lover, and the pressures of law school were gaining on me. The darkness in my heart must have come to the surface because as I walked by a destitute street person he turned to me and said, "It can't be that bad." Simple words that changed my life and brought the spirit back to my form.

❀ – ★ – ❀ – ★ – ❀ – ★ – ❀

When we think we're separate, we lose power. Whenever I say "my," I have lost my power. Power is not my power. . . . It is only gainable as part of a larger whole. Then you communicate with the rest of yourself—which may be a tree. You, reciprocally, are moved by the universe. Whenever you shut down connectedness, you get depressed. . . . It's fearful to know we're connected to everything in the universe, because then we're responsible.

—GLENDA TAYLOR

❀ – ⭐ – ❀ – ⭐ – ❀ – ⭐ – ❀

The Eye Opener

I was living in Chicago and going through what was a particularly cold winter both in my personal life and the outside temperature. One evening I was walking home from a bar where I had been drinking alone, feeling sorry for myself, when I saw a homeless man standing over an exhaust grate in front of a department store. He was wearing a filthy sport coat and approaching everyone who passed by for money.

I was too immersed in my own troubles to deal with him so I crossed the street. As I went by, I looked over and saw a businessman come out of the store and pull a ski parka out of a bag and hand it to the homeless man. For a moment both the man and I were frozen in time as the businessman turned and walked away. Then the man looked across the street at me. He shook his head slowly and I knew he was crying. It was the last time I have ever been able to disappear into my own sorrow.

My wife was dying of cancer. There were lots of non-random kindnesses in our lives. People who knew us did many ordinary and extraordinary things. But what touched many of us in our community happened early in my wife's struggle. We decided to have a water filtration system installed in our house to take the impurities out of the water. The plumber we contacted installed the system and wouldn't accept any payment. We found out later his father had died of cancer.

There is a love like a small lamp, which goes out when the oil is consumed; or like a stream which dries up when it doesn't rain. But there is a love that is like a mighty spring gushing up out of the earth; it keeps flowing forever, and is inexhaustible.

—ISAAC OF NINEVEH

PAYBACK

I had an older neighbor who was very kind to me, a father figure really. After he died, I noticed that his yard had become completely overgrown; his widow was not physically able to do the gardening. So one morning, after I saw her leave for the day, I jumped the fence and put in a few hours of work. It was my way of paying him back for the care he had taken of me.

*It is one of the most beautiful
compensations of life that no man
can sincerely try to help another
without helping himself.*

—Ralph Waldo Emerson

Practice Random Acts of Kindness!

- Visit a neighbor with a bouquet of flowers for no reason at all.

- Send a letter to a teacher you once had letting her know about the difference she made in your life.

- Say "Thank you" to someone who helps you and really mean it. You might want to look into his eyes, smile, and, if he is wearing a name tag say his name as well.

Buy a cold drink for your entire row at the baseball game.

Ask an older person to tell you a story about his or her youth, such as what her favorite song was and why, or how he met his spouse.

Let the person behind you in line at the grocery store go ahead of you.

Take out an ad in your local weekly newspaper thanking a tree, a park, a stream, a sunset, for giving you comfort.

CORPORATE KINDNESS

I am a corporate lawyer, and several years ago I was at my first closing. The investment banker came to deliver a check for $55 million to my client, and before my client arrived, I went to the Xerox machine to copy the check for our records. I put the check in the feeder of the copier, and it promptly shredded it! I told the banker about the mutilated check, and a moment later my client arrived, eager to receive the money. The banker looked at me and said to the client, "I can't believe it! I forgot the check!" He left and returned an hour later with a new check and I kept my job.

Our lives are fed by kind words and gracious behavior. We are nourished by expressions like "Excuse me," and other such simple courtesies. . . . Rudeness, the absence of the sacrament of consideration, is but another mark that our time-is-money society is lacking in spirituality, if not also in its enjoyment of life.

—ED HAYS

THE CAR ANGEL

I had just quit a job I hated and was determined to find a way to live that felt right. Money was very tight and my car was dying on me—I mean really falling apart. A friend gave me the name of a guy who lived close to me and fixed cars. So I took my wreck to him and he fixed it. I mean he fixed everything—working on it for two days and charging me only $60. The parts alone had to have cost him quite a bit more than that! It was almost as though he read into my soul: "This girl doesn't have money, and she need this car." He didn't know me from

Adam. That car was my vehicle for getting to where I needed to go and this total stranger made that possible when I really needed it.

Through our willingness to help others we can learn to be happy rather than depressed.

—GERALD JAMPOLSKY

COMPETITIVE KINDNESS

When I was in high school, I started playing field hockey. Since this was on the West Coast, there were no organized men's leagues, and we would more often than not end up playing college teams or adult club teams. One day we played the local university team which included one of the best field hockey players in the country. They killed us. I remember running around like mad, exerting massive amounts of energy while this one guy just glided around, past, and through us to score whenever he wanted. After the game I was sitting on the ground trying to catch my breath when the star walked over and started talking to me. For a while he just talked, going into all the intricacies of the game; he spoke to me as if I were an equal, as if I already understood all the things he was saying. After I had finally caught my breath, he took me back out on the field and spent an hour showing me various moves and tactics. I know it sounds silly, but even though the words were all about field hockey, the feeling it gave me was so much larger.

STRANDED

In the summer of 1977, a friend and I were driving in my 1967 VW bug to Ashland, Oregon, when my car threw a rod in the middle of nowhere on a Sunday (of course). We finally tracked down a tow truck driver who took the car to some swampy, willowy grove by the ocean—a wonderful place of rest, a kind of car heaven.

Meanwhile, however, we were completely stuck in this godforsaken place, at least until some means of transportation could be found when businesses opened up again on Monday. So the tow truck driver took us to his wonderful little woodsy home in the Mendocino mountains, fed us, and put us up for the night. Wonderful!

Each small task of everyday life is part of the total harmony of the universe.

—St. Thérèsa of Lisieux

NEIGHBORLY KINDNESS

For years, the Oakland, California, neighbors watched as Mary's house and yard slowly decayed. Mary was an elderly, wheelchair-bound widow who could no longer manage the necessary repairs and maintenance on her house. One day a couple of neighbors—a bus driver and an auto worker—went down to the city's Office of Community Development, got forty-five gallons of Mary's favorite-colored paint and a handful of painting supplies, and set to work. By the time they had finished, they had also put in a new lawn, cut back the tangled shrubs, and topped off the paint job with eye-catching trim.

> *Little kindnesses . . . will broaden your heart, and slowly you will habituate yourself to helping your fellow man in many ways.*
>
> —ZADIK

A Cup of Coffee

My grandmother was born in Russia at a time of great confusion and instability. She emigrated to this country as a young girl and ended up marrying a man who was extraordinarily successful. She could have lived in the fanciest neighborhood and eaten only at the best restaurants; instead she lived in a very modest area and would go to Woolworth's for coffee. In those days, a cup of coffee cost five cents, and whenever my grandmother would buy a cup, she would always leave a five-dollar tip. Her explanation was simple: "They work hard for their money."

True kindness presupposed the faculty of imagining as one's own the suffering and joy of others.

—ANDRE GIDE

GIVE AND YOU SHALL RECEIVE

I'm a doctor. Every day I come into the office and, probably like most doctors, slip into my professional caring role. I try hard to always be in a positive and attentive frame of mind for each and every one of my patients. But every now and then one of my patients will turn the tables on me and it is always such a genuinely touching thing. There I am, figuratively leaning forward, ready to be the one to do the giving, and out comes a bag of vegetables fresh from the garden, a coffee cake, a bouquet of home-grown flowers. The turn-around—the receiver

;iving to the giver—never fails to take
ne by surprise and always puts a large
;oofy grin on my face.

Kind words can be short and easy
to speak but their echoes are
truly endless.

—MOTHER TERESA

PRACTICE RANDOM ACTS OF KINDNESS!

• Make an anonymous donation to some local charity that is actively helping people—feeding the homeless, providing foster care for children, and so on. Or start a fund-raising drive in your office for such organizations.

• Slip a $20 bill into the pocketbook of a needy friend (or stranger).

• Organize your friends and workmates to gather their old clothes and give them to homeless people.

• Get a big piece of paper and a magi marker, and sit back to back with a

❀ – ☆ – ❀ – ☆ – ❀ – ☆ – ❀

·iend. Across the top of the page,
·rite the words physical, emotional,
esthetic, spiritual, and relational. Set
n alarm clock for ten minutes and
ake a thank-you card for all the peo-
le, places, or things that have affected
ou in those dimensions. When the
me is up, share your paper with one
nother.

Go to an AIDS hospice or hospital
·ard and see what you can do for one
erson.

Next time you go over a toll bridge
ay the toll for the car behind you and
on't forget to thank the toll taker.

THE GOOD FRIEND

A good friend and I had finally gotten together one evening after months of trying to make our schedules and the fifty miles separating us fit together somehow. We went out to eat and as usual had a great time talking about everything. I am always amazed at how quickly and deeply we reconnect even after months of barely speaking on the telephone.

While we were catching up on each other's lives, she noticed a man sitting alone at a table in the corner of the restaurant and commented to me that e looked sad, as if he were lacking for ompany. When we had finished our neal, I insisted on paying and my riend went along smiling. When the vaiter came to pick up the check, my riend told him that she would like to ay—anonymously—for the dinner of he man in the corner. I realized again vhy I cared about her so much.

No joy can equal the joy
of serving others.

—SAI BABA

TRUST

This is a story that's about fifty years old. During World War II, my father-in-law and his pregnant wife, who were living in Texas, wanted to visit with his parents in Oklahoma before he went to the Philippines. They had to drive back roads all the way. To their dismay, they had a flat and no spare tire. Walking several deserted miles, they finally came to a farmhouse. Now this was in the days when rubber was rationed, but the farmer who lived there took off a tire from his car and said, "Drive into town, get your tire fixed, and leave nine at the gas station. I'll get my tire back later on." His trusting action really saved the day for my in-laws.

I try to give to the poor people for love what the rich could get for money. No. I wouldn't touch a leper for a thousand pounds, yet I willingly cure him for the love of God.

—MOTHER TERESA

PRACTICE RANDOM ACTS OF KINDNESS!

• If someone in your neighborhood leaves on a trip and forgets to stop the newspaper, pick them up and put them in a safe out-of-view spot.

• Next time you go to the movies, pick out someone behind you in the line and tell the ticket seller you want to pay for their ticket as well. Make sure to ask that they not reveal who paid for their ticket.

• If you know someone who is going through a bad day or a difficult time in life, make it better by doing something—anything—to let him or her know someone cares . . . and don't let on who did it!

• Laugh out loud often and share your smile generously.

• Praise the work or attitude of a person you work with to someone else in the office in a time, place, and manner that is outside of all office politics.

• If you are the boss, bring your secretary a cup of coffee in the morning.

• Buy gift cards and give them—anonymously—to people you think could really use them.

THE HILLS OF SAN FRANCISCO

You hear stories about tourists trying to drive in San Francisco all the time. I discovered a whole new twist one day when I was walking up a particularly steep hill and saw a car stopped near the top with a very frightened woman inside. As I watched, she made a few attempts to get moving but each time seemed to lose more ground than she gained. Then a man came out of the corner market. The next thing I know, she gets out of the car and goes around to the passenger side while he climbs into the driver's seat and promptly drives the car up over the top of the dreaded hill. By then, I had reached the store where the helpful man's wife was standing, watching the proceedings. She told me that her husband, who owns the market, has been doing that for years, and that during the summer-time—peak tourist season—he will "rescue" as many as ten scared drivers a week.

Miracles occur naturally as expressions of love. The real miracle is the love that inspires them. In this sense everything that comes from love is a miracle.

—A Course in Miracles

WEEPING WILLOWS

When I was in high school, I had a friend who asked me to help him plant some weeping willow trees down by a creek. It seems that he had watched every year as the banks of this creek had been increasingly eaten away. It had gotten to the point where the water was threatening to overflow into the nearby housing development. My friend had obviously done his research; he found out that willows grew quickly, easily, and with a great spreading root system that drinks up lots of water which would stabilize the creek bank. When I met him at the creek, he had a huge bundle of willow branches in his arms. We spent most of the day planting these willow sprigs up and down the endangered curve.

Many years later, I was home visiting and found myself walking down by that creek. Where we spent that afternoon is now a beautiful idyllic bend with a long curving row of large graceful willows bending out over the water.

SERVICE WITH A SMILE

I was out to dinner with a friend and we ended up talking for a while with our waitress. She was one of those waitresses who was such a pleasure she made the whole dining experience that much more enjoyable. She told us about how she was working two jobs and trying to put herself through school at night.

It was not a very expensive restaurant, and I think our total bill was less than $20. But when we paid, we left her a $100 tip. What a great feeling.

The great, dominant, all controlling fact of this life is the innate bias of the human spirit, not towards evil, as the theologists tell us, but towards good. But for that bias, man would never have been man; he would only have been one more species of wild animal ranging a savage, uncultivated globe, the reeking battleground of sheer instinct and appetite.

—WILLIAM ARCHER

HELPING A FRIEND IN NEED

There was a time in my life when everything was working so smoothly, I found myself sitting at home one Saturday with all my work done, all my household chores completed: dishes washed, laundry folded and put away, house dusted, grocery shopping completed, and that deliciou feeling of having nothing to do. Then I thought about a friend from work who was a single mother of two small children and never seemed to have th time for anything. I jumped into my car, drove over to her house, walked,

n and said, "Put me to work." At first
he didn't really believe it, but we
ended up having a great time, cleaning
ike mad, taking time out to feed and
play with the kids, and then diving
back into the chores.

*Charity is the bone shared with
the dog when you are just as
hungry as the dog.*

—JACK LONDON

❀ – ⭐ – ❀ – ⭐ – ❀ – ⭐ – ❀

Practice Random Acts of Kindness!

• Take the opportunity in conversations with friends to tell them about kindnesses you have experienced and ask about their experiences. Just talking about acts of kindness brings them alive in the world.

• Get your children to go through their toys and put aside those they want to donate to children who are less fortunate.

• Next time you go to the ice cream parlor, pay for a few free cones to be given to the next kids to come in.

❀ – ✪ – ❀ – ✪ – ❀ – ✪ – ❀

If you have an infirm person living near you, offer to do the grocery shopping for him or her.

Pick up the mail for a senior or someone else who could use the assistance.

If there is a garden you pass frequently and enjoy, stop by one day and leave a note letting the occupants know how much pleasure their garden gives you.

Make a dedication on your local radio station to all those people who smiled at strangers today.

A human being is a part of the whole that we call the universe, a part limited in time and space. He experiences himself, his thoughts and feelings, as something separated from the rest— a kind of optical illusion of his consciousness. This illusion is a prison for us, restricting us to our personal desires and to affection for only the few people nearest us. Our task must be to free ourselves from this prison by widening our circle of compassion to embrace all living beings and all of nature.

—ALBERT EINSTEIN